Richard Boylston Hall

Every Man his own Farrier

Common-Sense Instructions for Shoeing Horses

Richard Boylston Hall

Every Man his own Farrier
Common-Sense Instructions for Shoeing Horses

ISBN/EAN: 9783744730778

Printed in Europe, USA, Canada, Australia, Japan

Cover: Foto ©Andreas Hilbeck / pixelio.de

More available books at **www.hansebooks.com**

EVERY MAN HIS OWN FARRIER.

COMMON-SENSE INSTRUCTIONS FOR

SHOEING HORSES

BALANCING TROTTER, PACER, RUNNER

WITHOUT AID OF MECHANICAL APPLIANCES.

R. BOYLSTON HALL,

EXPERT FARRIER,

307 RIALTO BUILDING, CHICAGO, ILL.

9 State Street Room 43. Boston Ill.

CONTRIBUTOR TO

SPIRIT OF THE TIMES, NEW YORK CITY.
KENTUCKY STOCK FARM, LEXINGTON.
AMERICAN HORSE BREEDER, BOSTON.
THE WESTERN HORSEMAN, INDIANAPOLIS.
WEEKLY HORSE WORLD, BUFFALO.
THE LIVERY STABLE, NEW YORK CITY.
RURAL WORLD, ST. LOUIS.
BREEDER AND SPORTSMAN, SAN FRANCISCO

N. B.—Any special cases of peculiar action, irregular, fatiguing and interfering with proper and rhythmical motion, that may seem to be too complicated to be corrected by instructions contained in the following pages, can have the attention of the author either by mail—form of information required in such cases is printed on pages 66 and 67 —or personally at regularly stipulated prices to be made known upon application at his office or by correspondence. He will visit any point in the country on satisfactory terms.

ESTABLISHED 1872.

ZERO MARX SIGN WORKS

(INCORPORATED.)

Signs of Every Description.

OFFICE AND FACTORY:

160-162 E. Superior Street,

TELEPHONE 1031 NORTH.   CHICAGO.

ZERO MARX
MIRROR AND SHOCK CO.

WE MANUFACTURE

Mirrors and Shocks,

Mirror Signs, Mirror Novelties, Etc.
Re-Silvering Old Mirrors.

OFFICE AND FACTORY:

160=162 E. Superior Street,
CHICAGO.

(Mention this Book.)

CONTENTS.

" *Truth crushed to earth shall rise again,—*
The eternal years of God are hers;
But Error, wounded, writhes with pain,
And dies among his worshippers."

TO

My Good Wife,

MY BEST FRIEND,

THIS BOOK

IS AFFECTIONATELY DEDICATED

BY

THE AUTHOR.

INTRODUCTION.

Having been importuned by many friends and for many years to publish a book on Farriery and Horseshoeing, I have finally concluded to do so. Recognizing full well that it costs time and money to properly prepare such a work, for there are so many kinds of feet of horses, dissimilar often only in so slight a degree, that my fear has been it would require too large a volume to contain the necessary information and directions so plainly expressed, and written—"that he who runs may read"—so as to be easily and readily understood by all who would require such information. It shall be the aim of this book of instruction to avoid, as nearly as possible, technical and high sounding words or phrases, and to keep down to commonplace horseshoer's talk, with proper regard to giving plainly and fully all necessary directions to govern in the preparation and shoeing of any and all of the many different sorts of feet that may occur to the writer; endeavoring not to let slip any of the many peculiar ones that have come under his eye in his long and varied experience.

Farriery.

Webster's definition of a Farrier is a "Shoer of a horse." As practiced in his day his duties were, apparently, only the paring of the foot and the nailing on of the iron shoe. But now it carries with it a broader meaning, it has become an Art; the understanding of the motor power of the horse, directing the preparation of the foot and so adjusting its angle to the limb it supports as to conform strictly to Nature's Laws of Propulsion, form the most important duties of the Farrier; next in importance are the directions given the smith as to the fitting of the shoe to the foot after it has been made ready to receive it. Thus it will be seen that the art of Farriery is not merely paring the foot and making and nailing on the shoe. It is therefore important, in fact necessary, that every Owner and Breeder should fully understand Farriery, and this work is published for the sole purpose of imparting such information; hence the title, **"Every Man His Own Farrier."**

By far the most important matters in connection with the proper preparation and shoeing of the feet, as explained in these pages, will be such as apply more particularly to light harness and carriage horses. Quite a deal of attention will be given to the "Balancing of the Trotter, Pacer and Runner" for speed purposes. The extra attention is not given to the class of horses mentioned to the detriment of the comfort of those that "work for a living" as it were, for they will receive proper consideration herein, but because the more rapid action of the former make them more amenable to the many forms of lamenesses that afflict *too large a percentage* of our horses—afflictions almost invariably traceable to their unbalanced and improperly shod feet. One point it seems important to make emphasis of right here is: *Never undertake to obtain what is called a "seating" for the shoe on the foot, by applying it hot. The shoe should never be applied to the foot of the animal when too hot for the smith to hold in his hand.*

Something that Mr. Robert Bonner Says.

In a paper read at the dinner of the New York Farmers recently by Mr. Robert Bonner, that gentleman says: "I have been often asked why is it trainers and blacksmiths know so little about shoeing? * * Because they know nothing, generally speaking, of the anatomy of the foot and have no disposition to give the requisite time to acquiring a knowledge of it. Besides they are too old to learn. It is to the rising generation that we must look for improvement in this line. In my experience I have found that while old trainers and blacksmiths may appreciate two or three new points about the horse's foot, you will make them, with a very few exceptions, angry with you and disgusted with themselves by giving them too many valuable points—points which they can neither comprehend nor 'digest.' The result of this will be that they will feel like abandoning the study of the whole subject as being too intricate and complicated."

The sole object of this work is to instruct the present, as also the "rising generation," in plain language —avoiding as far as possible the use of all "*hard words*"—how comparatively easy it is to acquire a thorough knowledge of the anatomy of the foot and how to shoe it, to fit the horse to perform with comfort, all the duties his master, man, requires of him. Not to antagonize the trainers and blacksmiths but to give them some points of information that may be, some of them at least, new to them. This book is a pocket manual and can be readily referred to to assist them, possibly, upon some points on which they may be in doubt.

Breeders and Owners.

Every breeder and owner of horses should understand farriery and horseshoeing. It will be found of great benefit to their stock, and of consequent pecuniary advantage to themselves to possess sufficient knowledge on these points to be enabled to put such into practical use, with the resultant advantages promised from careful practice of the many beneficial points to be learned, and which the author of this work, from his many years of study and practice, feels confident he can give *plainly* and *fully* and will endeavor to do so and in language easily understood.

Feet of Foals.

The class to whom this article is addressed will best conserve their interests as "breeders and owners," by giving quite a considerable portion of their time and attention to that most important matter, the keeping of the feet of their foals carefully looked after while they are still sucklings. When they shall have become say about four to five weeks old, yes, even younger than that, if any irregularity of growth shall have been discovered, the farrier (horseshoer) should be called to the farm and the youngsters' feet should all be looked over and the rasp brought into use to true and balance them if requisite; at this stage of growth nothing but the rasp will be needed, the knife not being necessary. If this important part of the duties of the careful breeder are judiciously attended to, then, when the foals are ready to go into the hands of the smith to be regularly shod, he will have but little to do except smooth off their feet and adjust the shoes.

Shoes Removed Every Three Weeks.

Now, then, comes up another and fully as important a point in the matter of keeping the feet of the colts, and maturer animals, trued, balanced, in proper proportion and in proper angle to the limbs they support, so that the articulation shall be as near smooth and frictionless as possible, and that is, never allow the shoes to remain on the feet longer than *three weeks*, when they should be removed, reset, or new ones put on, as the case may require. The importance of this is obvious. The feet in a healthy state of growth, grow about three-eighths ($\frac{3}{8}$″) of an inch each month and they grow irregularly, therefore, to keep the animal "*plumb on his pins*," advantage must be taken of the irregularities of growth by observing the rule pointed out, as to duration of time the shoes should remain on the feet, without removal.

TO THE READER.

After reading over the pages of this work carefully, examining the illustrations, etc., please acknowledge receipt and write on postal card, sent under cover with book, your opinion of it, and oblige,

Very respectfully,

THE AUTHOR.

Chicago Horse, Harness

AND . . .

Carriage Exchange

1629 to 1637 Wabash Ave.,   CHICAGO, ILL.

Incorporated, Capital Stock $100,000.00, Full Paid.

OFFICERS.

ALEX'R MacKAY, PRESIDENT.

DR. D. A. K. STEELE, VICE-PRESIDENT.

JAS. D. LYNCH, SECRETARY AND TREASURER

Reference, National Bank of the Republic, Chicago.

This company has unequaled facilities for the sale of High Class Horses. Its location in the business center enables purchasers to step in at any time on their way to and from business, to examine the animals offered for sale and they have the option of buying at auction or privately.

Breeders and dealers are invited to ship their stock to this Exchange where they will find the best stabling accommodations and largest show-ring ever constructed for the sale of horses. Public auctions Tuesday and Saturday of each week. Honest dealing guaranteed. A cordial invitation is extended to sellers and buyers to make this Exchange their headquarters. All business strictly on commission. Correspondence solicited.

(Mention this Book.)

11

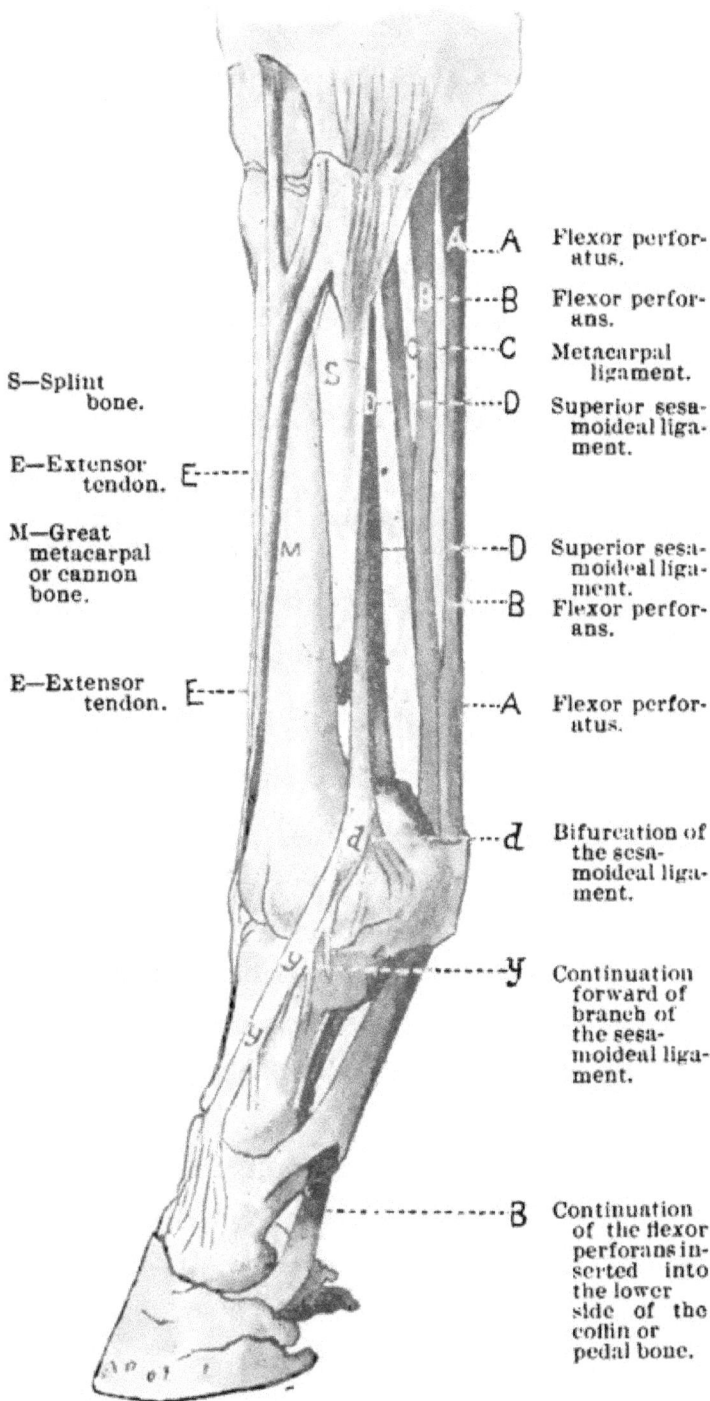

A .... Flexor perforatus.

B .... Flexor perforans.

C .... Metacarpal ligament.

D .... Superior sesamoideal ligament.

S—Splint bone.

E—Extensor tendon.

M—Great metacarpal or cannon bone.

E—Extensor tendon.

D .... Superior sesamoideal ligament.

B .... Flexor perforans.

A .... Flexor perforatus.

d .... Bifurcation of the sesamoideal ligament.

y .... Continuation forward of branch of the sesamoideal ligament.

B .... Continuation of the flexor perforans inserted into the lower side of the coffin or pedal bone.

Draper and Tailor

AUDITORIUM ANNEX,

222 MICHIGAN AVENUE, CHICAGO, ILL.

- - - - - - -

THE author takes pleasure in inserting the advertisement of his friend

JOE DAY . . . . .

and as " JOE " has left it to him to say what he chooses, he is pleased to say:

JOE

keeps abreast of the times, is broad-gauged, "up to date," and is always the first to have in stock the latest novelties of cut and pattern. The only trouble with his clothes is, they won't wear out, inside or outside, for the linings and trimmings correspond in texture and durability with the stuff the garments are cut from.

When you come to this great city, call and see " Joe " and tell him you read what his friend Hall said.

General Instructions and Comments.

One of the first essentials for the smith—the horse-shoer—to enable him to practice, with the desired success, on the points laid down in these instructions, is a fairly smooth level floor to his shop. If he has not such, and cares not to go to the expense of laying one, he can have a platform made, say about 10 feet by 5 feet, that he can use as he wishes, and place at one side when not required for use. This certainly would not put him to great expense. Have such a platform made of fairly clear stuff, that is, free from knots, so that it will wear and keep comparatively smooth.

Abusing Horses at the Shop.

Patience is a virtue and an essential for a horse-shoer. Remember it is a dumb animal that is being dealt with: he cannot talk and inform the smith that it hurts him to stand on one foot while he is preparing the other and opposite one to be shod. The crowding on the nerves at the base affects the whole nerve system to its entire centre and the poor animal is in the same nervous condition that human beings often are. Therefore, be patient in the work of shoeing their feet and *under no circumstances ever strike a horse in the shoeing shop and particularly never about the head.* Firmness, but kindness, will accomplish more than harsh treatment. The natural disposition of the horse is to do what is right and in nearly all cases where they do not behave well, it arises from having been abused, or from not having been taught to understand what is wanted of them. It may at times be necessary to use a "twitch" on the nose of restive colts and nervous horses, but don't abuse the use of it and don't abuse them in any way.

Regular Form for Shoes.

When the feet are fairly sound, true and level, needing no peculiar style of shoes, always shoe them with a plain shoe of even thickness from heel to heel, the hind feet as well as the fore ones, except in "sharpening."

One of the errors of horseshoe making, in nearly *all* machine as also most of the hand-made ones, is that of turning them thicker at the heels than in the front of the shoe. This is wrong; the front part of the shoe wears away the fastest, therefore, as the foot is supposed to be level when the shoe is adjusted, this irregular wear is gradually throwing it out of level. By having the shoe of even thickness when first placed on the foot, this irregular wear is not productive of much evil, as far as the shoe itself is responsible.

Calkins, How to Proportion.

Calkins are rarely needed for the shoes of our light harness and carriage horses, for either foot—that is, not even for the hind ones—except for the snow path in winter. When calkins are used on the shoes they should be placed as follows: The toe calkins, all of them, back across the inside of the web of the shoe, and they should not be made too long, from side to side, never over one and one-half inches in length. They should not be made too deep (say about one-half of an inch for the toe calkins and three-eighths [⅜″] of an inch for those at the heels) ; the toe calkins should always be made deeper in proportion than those for the heels, say as about four (4) parts of depth at the toe to three (3) parts at the heels; that is, the depth of the shoes, calkins included, must be, at the heels, about three-fourths of that of the front. This will assist in equalizing the wear and prove a strong feature in the tendency to keep the ground lay of the feet level.

Proper Manner of Nail Driving.

As a general rule to be observed in nailing the shoes to the feet the nails should never be driven too far back—except in some case or cases that will be mentioned in this volume—they should never be driven into the wall of the foot back of a point just a shade in front of the line of the wings of the coffin or pedal bone. Nails driven back of this point will bind the foot together at the only point where Nature has arranged to give it a spring, or easement, to the blow on the ground. These are general ideas of nail driving to govern in the ordinary routine of horshoeing; special cases will be treated by themselves.

In making the nail holes in the shoe, it is better, for many reasons, to punch each hole by itself and properly countersink on the ground surface to obtain a firm seating for the heads. When the shoe is creased for the holes, the nails have more play, are more apt, therefore, to break and the shoe is also weakened. This manner of construction will be found to be the rule on any and all the shoes shown in this work and it is, unquestionably, the more correct way.

The wall of the hind different from that of the fore foot is the thickest and strongest at the back part, nails can, therefore—when necessary to retain a firmer hold for the shoe and to prevent a not infrequent accident, that of their spreading at the heels—be driven further back towards the heels without seriously interfering with the natural expansion of the foot.

Clips Rarely Necessary.

Clips on shoes should rarely or never be used. Shoes can scarcely be fitted properly with clips on them; they are a device fit only for the careless and hurried smith who uses them rather than take a little more time and properly fit the shoes to the feet. There are feet that require the use of clips on the shoes and on such they *must be used*, as will be explained under the proper heading, in describing the class of feet to which they are necessary.

The Sole.

The sole should not be removed from the foot —for it sheds at proper time—only so much of it as is immediately under the shoe, to avoid its pressing on it.

About the Frog.

The frog may be left untouched, except that it shall show any evidence of thrush, when it should be carefully cleaned out at the crevice and at the sides, thus removing all diseased parts so that any remedies it may be thought proper to apply shall have opportunity to act. Also the ragged edges of any diseased frog should be cleaned off so as not to afford a lodgment for deleterious substances. The frog is a cushion placed under the navicular bone and joint of that name to ease the action at that point as also that of the flexor tendon that passes under the navicular and fastens on to the coffin or pedal bone. Its India-rubber-like consistency, which is its condition when in health, fully justifies this definition of its use, and experience has shown that to be its office; it exerts no influence by *itself whatever* in *expanding* or *contracting* the foot.

The Bars.

The same may be said of the bars; they do not in any way prevent contraction or prevent expansion. They are placed there as a strength-giving support to the "horny box," the foot, the same as are the walls that they assimilate so nearly to in texture. They should not therefore be removed only to such an extent that they do not protrude below the surface lay of the wall and need not necessarily have any bearing on the shoe. In fact, in the case of contracted feet care should be taken that they do not bear on the shoe, as they would thus force the commissures up into the sensitive foot, hurting the animal as would the nails of a man's boot heels forced through the inner sole and pushing up against his foot heel.

The Frog Again.

Now having defined the duties of the frog, it must be seen that it must always be free to "give and take" as it were; it must *never, therefore, under any circumstances* be confined by a bar across the heels of the shoe, by using what is commonly called one of the most pernicious inventions, a "bar shoe." Neither must it have a concussive blow. For two reasons this last is wrong:

First. To properly perform the duties laid down for and required of it, it should not be subjected to any jarring blow that can be avoided by properly preparing the foot so that its surface shall not be too close to the ground.

Second. It is rarely that a foot will be found where the heels can be pared down to so slight a depth as to afford the so-called "frog pressure," (most absurd nonsense) that they will not be so low as to throw the articulation all out of gear and cause serious trouble to it; as also more or less injury to the tendons and muscles.

Irregular Action.

All irregular action of the limbs and feet must be attributed, almost invariably, to a want of balance in the foot or feet. Therefore, to correct faulty action look carefully at the base to ascertain what causes the trouble. Never undertake to correct such evils by more weight of iron on one side of the foot than on the other, or by more thickness of iron, except in the rarest of cases—and such necessity will be shown in these pages—at one point of the shoe than at another. All such artificial attempts at correcting faulty articulation will result in dire injury to the motor power of the animal and *must be strenuously avoided under any and all circumstances.* Examine carefully, at all times, as directed, the base of the machinery, for the motor power of the horse is *live machinery,* and must be treated on the same plane of scientific mechanics as any other machinery.

Level Floor.

Now, with reference to the use of the smooth level floor. This is required so that the horse shall be able to stand as plumb as it is possible for him to do so, having nothing in the way of an uneven floor to make him stand otherwise. This is necessary; for in order to true and balance his feet,the eye of the smith must be cast up and down the front line of each leg to ascertain if the line of the centre of the leg would meet a line drawn through the centre of the foot from front to back of such foot, for no man living can true and balance the foot of a horse by looking at and around the surface, while the foot is held back of the leg and in hand. When the foot shall look to be true and balanced from viewing the leg and foot from the front, then stand at the side of the animal, or rather a little way off, and judge if the bearing of the limb shall look to be in a comfortable position in the foot from that standpoint of observation. If so you have now the foot prepared to receive the shoe.

Directions for fitting the shoes will be found in their proper places. as describing the various sorts of fitting for the many variety of foot shapes.

Let the Smith Live.

Remember. owners, the most important of all things, as regards utilizing the best efforts of your horses, is to give the most painstaking care to their feet and the shoeing of them, therefore let the smith have a chance to live. Employ his services as often as they shall be needed. Pay him a fair price for the use you make of his time and skill and you will be the winner "by a large majority." Penuriousness in this respect will be found to be expensive economy.

Particular Care of Feet.

There is no need of anxiety on the score of colts and horses not receiving sufficient food and of good quality, but there is cause for much anxiety as to a continuous state of health of the motor powers of the animals, so they shall be ready and willing, at all times, to perform the tasks their master, man, may set for them. The much neglected *care of their feet* should receive, by far, the most careful attention, too much stress *cannot be laid on this all-important duty.*

Nature's Protection.

Never cover up the foot, or any of it, on its ground surface, more than what space a *narrow* webbed shoe will cover. The foot requires and must have, at all times, a free circulation of air *all around it.* Therefore, never use pads, tar, oakum and such things. Leave the sole—Nature's protection—in the foot and it is a better protection than the ingenuity of man has ever yet, or ever will, discover.

The Foot Needs No "Protection."

The foot does not need the nailing on to it of a shoe for "*protection*," as in the generally accepted meaning of that term. Leave the bars and sole untouched and it makes no difference how hard the roads, or how rough. Nature has prepared the foot to stand any blow it gets on the ground at any rate of speed. All the shoe is for, and that is why it should always be narrow-webbed, is to protect the wall from breaking and from wearing away—at the work man cuts out for the animal—faster than Nature can reproduce it. The narrow webbed shoe is the most desirable for obvious reasons; in the first place, as explained, it protects all of that part of the foot—the wall—that it is at all needful to protect, then again the wide webbed shoe must necessarily be heavier, consequently the blow on the ground is heavier, producing that "stinging" effect so much talked about by trainers and drivers. There is a vibrative, concussive blow to the sole of the foot from the use of wide webbed shoes that is jarring and painful, and that it cannot get from the narrow webbed ones, for they do not extend to the inner surface of the foot over the sole. No harm can happen to the animal's foot, if it is in a healthy state of growth and properly balanced, to have it go unshod—provided the sharp edge of the wall is rounded off with the rasp to prevent it from breaking when coming in contact with the ground—the animal can as well perform any rational duties set for him. But then, of course, this work is to instruct how to *properly shoe* the foot and it shall be the aim of the author to carry out, fully, the requirements.

Proper Bedding to Keep Feet Cool.

In many stables, more particularly in the western country here, it is customary to use pine waste, shavings, sawdust, etc., for bedding. On the score of the economy of first cost, this is excusable, but on no other, and where it is used as a bedding for the horse it should not be allowed to remain in the stall during the daytime for him to stand on, as it is creative of much fever in the feet. The animal had much better stand on the plain floor, and this will not be fatiguing to him, if his feet are kept in a healthy state, and it will be the endeavor of this work to give necessary instructions, looking to that end. Straw is infinitely better, but it should be kept fresh and sweet. The best of all materials known to the author, and he has had considerable experience in its use, is sand, the ocean sand, or the sand from our large lakes, and he never knew one of his horses to have fever in its feet when using it. His horses were "bedded" with it, no straw being used in addition, they slept on the sand, sometimes with, and sometimes without blankets. It was raked over carefully on top to remove the manure that had been dropped, and replenished with fresh every few weeks, about every two or three weeks. his memory seems to suggest.

Walking Exercise.

This work is not intended to give instruction in training and driving, but one thing the author will say, as the outcome of experience from carefully and thoroughly testing its efficacy, and that is that the best exercise to impart strength to the general system, to promote growth of muscle, muscle that is supple and healthy, and make speed, is walking exercise, *fast*, *very fast* walking, with a boy weighing say 125 lbs. on the back. Not dubbing along but get all of the horses that are in training so that they can walk faster than 4 miles in one hour (the author had one that walked a mile in 10 minutes) and walk them over other day 3 to 4 miles. Every trainer and driver should understand farriery and horseshoeing and they do not fully understand the *art* of training and driving unless they possess knowledge on these, the most important of all the duties belonging to the trade, as it may be called.

"Corns."

There is no such thing as a "Corn" in the foot of the horse, but the author will explain certain things in connection with this misapplied term, as shall enable a proper treatment of the foot said to be thus afflicted. The discoloration of the sole, at the point at the back part of the foot between the bar and wall, is caused by a deposit of extravasated blood, bruised blood, commonly speaking.

The cause of this is an excessive tightness around the coronet, the blood gets into the foot, but the small veins become so congested that it cannot make its round of circulation, as it were, and get out again; it is therefore the bursting of these small veins that causes their contents to trickle down and lodge in the lowest point of the foot at the place where the discoloration makes its appearance. The small veins can be, and are, occasionally broken with the same consequence, discoloration of the sole, by the foot being too broad and weak, though such cases are so rare as to scarcely need attention, but will be explained however.

Explanation.

There is no discomfort to the animal at the point where this deposit is made apparent, and there is, therefore, nothing gained by cutting away the sole there, and above all things, never, under any circumstances, should any foreign substance be injected into the foot after the foolish operation of cutting away the sole has been resorted to, as is too often done. The author has seen a temporary relief given to the animal by cutting a piece out of the wall at the point opposite to where appears this discoloration, so that the wall at that point has no bearing on the shoe. But as mentioned, this is only a temporary relief. The way to relieve this foot of its tightened condition at the coronet is to put it into proper proportion, which will be explained, so that the bones of the foot, that have been crowded up out of their proper resting place, can be let down, as it were, into the foot, where they properly belong, instead of being crowded up into the coronet. The author has seen horses that came to the shop lame, from so-called corns, go sound before they had gotten a quarter of a mile from the shop, by relieving the coronet as suggested, without doing anything else to the foot, or placing upon it anything but a plain shoe. For some insight into the manner of treating a foot so afflicted, see direction under No. 14.

Quarter Cracks.

These are caused also by the tightness at the coronet resulting from the same unnatural position of the bones of the feet. The cracking of the wall at the quarter is the best thing that could happen, under the circumstances. The tightly bound foot opens, so to speak, and the animal experiences a relief, and if now placed in the hands of an expert farrier, he can soon increase his comfort,and do so in a rational way, which will not be by using that most pernicious contrivance, the "bar shoe;" a device never to be used. The author has removed such shoes from the feet and has found the frog, underneath the pernicious bar, rotted away with thrush.

Articulation.

Care must be taken in getting the articulation started correctly, much, if not all, depends on this important matter. The first joint of this live machinery of the motor power is made by the lower pastern or coronary bone, playing in the socket made to receive it in the pedal, or coffin bone, and the navicular bone that works in connection with these two.

When the foot is true, balanced, in proper proportion and in proper angle to the limb it supports, it is a sure indication that this foundation joint is in a perfectly true and scientifically correct mechanical position; consequently, barring a rare and infrequent accident, all the joints throughout the limb above will be found to be just as mechanically correct in their action. Per contra, if this foundation joint is wrong, making an uncomfortable articulation, with increased friction, such a condition is likely to be made manifest at most any point of articulation through the entire limb. Yes, even to interfering with the action at shoulders and quarters, affecting also, as it is most likely to do, the tendons and muscles as well.

Toeing Out and In.

These two faults are cause of more annoyance to horseshoers than all other troubles afflicting the fore feet. put together. Of course, what causes the one is almost directly opposite to that causing the other. Writers disagree on this point, and the author knows that he will be severely criticised for the statements he shall here make in regard to the cause of these faulty positions of the feet, but then he is used to such criticisms—or more particularly they may be called the opinions of faultfinders—so they do not in the least disturb him, particularly so, when his continued experience on the lines here laid down are satisfying in the highest degree. Some people claim that the foot points outward—"toes out"—because the elbow turns in towards the body, and per contra points inward—"toes in"—because the elbow turns outward, away from the body.

The ground taken in this work is that such theories are not correct, but that the position of the elbow is made to be what it is—relatively to the body—by the position of the foot on its surface lay, and that as it continues to turn out or in, more, the elbow will be affected in its position relatively in consequence. One writer, who is considered to be one of some eminence, claims that the cause of the foot toeing out, is its being too high on the inside heels and the contrary condition of the foot compels it to toe in. This work assumes a different ground. It claims that the toeing out foot will be found to be too high from the point of the outside heel, all along the outside of the foot to past the immediate point, a direct front, of the foot—though sometimes this increased depth may be noticeable only up to just short of the point of toe, and cease, in other cases, at the *outside* toe; though often the inside of the foot, from about the line of the wing of the coffin bone, back to the point of heel, will be found to be pushed up so that measured from point where wall and flesh join, at the inside heel, down to surface of wall, it will be found to be deeper than the opposite heel with like measurement.

The "toeing-in" foot will be found to be caused by the inside of such foot being too high, or too deep, rarely, almost never, will the outside heel seem to be affected, to correspond, in an opposite direction, to the effect just noticed of the inside heel as affecting the toeing-out foot. Now, there are no infallible rules to govern these two faulty positions, but in more than 95 out of 100 cases they will be found to be caused by the wrong proportion of the feet here laid down. Either of the faulty positions referred to, are cause of much annoyance to the animal, for they are productive of increased friction with consequent fatigue, therefore, lessened power to perform, at any gait, but more particularly emphasized as the rapidity of the gait increases; for it must be borne in mind that the line of this faulty action is the same at all rates of speed and does not change, as seems to be the very erroneous idea, because of the more rapid motion; proving the well-known fact that motion may be quicker than the eye, even at the rate of the speed-action of the feet and limbs of a horse, and particularly so in such a case, for the eye is confused by the action of two pieces of machinery, as the two fore feet, working in the same direction and so closely together.

In the proper place will be described how to prepare and shoe these two kinds of feet, to assist Nature in her wise endeavors to correct the faulty growth and establish once more true, smooth and comparatively frictionless articulation.

Contraction.

"Contracted feet," are of course more frequent with the fore than with the hind ones. Not necessary to go into an exhaustive explanation why this is so: let the fact remain and let the endeavor here be to correct the evils of contraction. How opposite do the fore and hind feet behave? The fore ones contract most frequently on the inside, while the hind ones are more likely to become contracted on the outside.

Toe Weights and Side Weights.

That irregular-gaited horses have been made to go more evenly with their use, it would be foolish to deny, for such is unquestionably true, but that injured joints, tendons and muscles have been made to pay the penalty of employing such agents, is equally true. The use of side weights rarely, if ever, are of any benefit in changing the line of action of the foot to which they are applied, unless some attention has been given also to the foot to improve the articulation. They are more apt to emphasize the faulty action and carry the foot further in its wrongly directed course, if the incorrect position of the foot is still allowed to maintain, and will surely bring, in such cases, injury to the motor power. If the feet are trued, balanced, in proper porportion and in proper angle to the limbs they support, the applying of weights to them of any kind will not be found essential to establish a true, rythmical action and the animal's gameness and disposition to do his best in fighting out his races will be manifest by the absence of such a handicap of weight-forcing appliances. Immediate results, sometimes, when races are on, may be an excuse for the use of weights, but as soon afterwards as the art of farriery can be brought to bear to assist nature in correcting the error of action, the horse should be taken in hand and the feet so balanced as to make the articulation correct, so that the animal's instinct shall suggest to him that the smooth, even gait is the most comfortable, and he therefore will naturally adhere to it.

Hopples or Hobbles.

The author unhesitatingly asserts that the use of the above named appliances can be dispensed with if the instructions contained in this work are carefully complied with, and with greatly increased comfort to the animal as also increased speed and gameness to fight out his races. He asserts this because he can understandingly do so from the fact that he has trued and balanced the feet of a *great many* that *could not go even and true without them* with the result of increas-

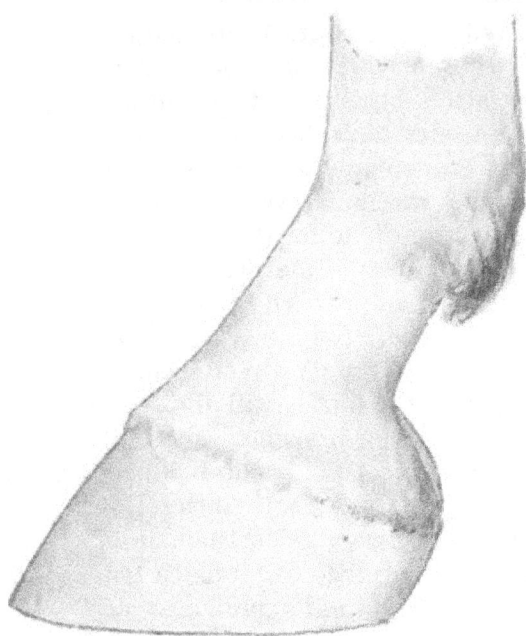

No. 1.

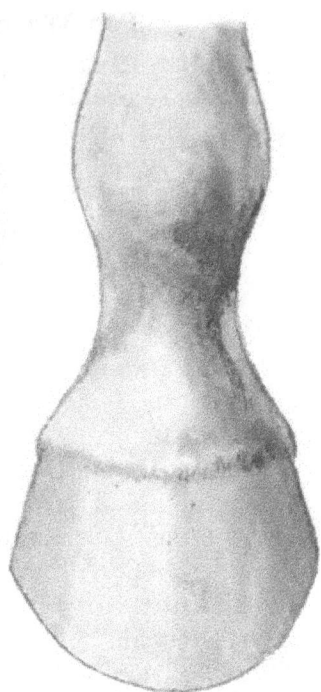

No. 3.

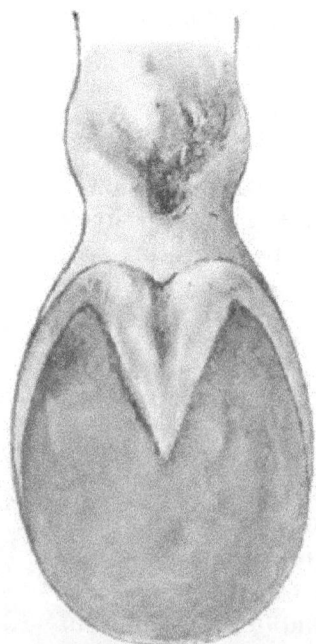

No. 2.

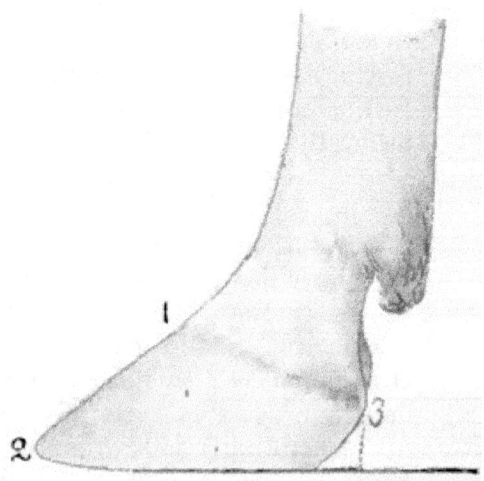

No. 4.

ing the speed and enabling the animals to go at a smooth and rhythmical gait as a consequence.

A Perfect Foot.

Numbers 1, 2 and 3 represent different views of the same foot. These views represent what might be called a foot of proper proportion and in proper angle to the limb it supports. If horses' feet can be kept in about such proportions and angle, the gait will be found to be rhythmical and true, with frictionless articulation. Care must be taken to fit the shoes to such a foot even with the wall all around and they should be made of even thickness from heel to heel with no calkins on either the fore or hind shoes, except it shall be necessary to sharpen for the snow path, when of course calkins must be used and placed on the shoes as instructed in the paragraph on the subject under the heading "Calkins, How to Proportion." When the feet are in such a degree of perfection of balance and proportion, light, narrow webbed shoes will be found to be all that are needed to keep the gait true and even, and the hind shoes should be made of the same bar of steel that the front ones are made of, when, if there shall be any difference in the size of the feet, as the hind ones on 'the same animal are sometimes found to be a trifle smaller than the fore ones, they will each be carrying their proper weight. Such difference will rarely or ever be found to be greater than about one-half to three-fourths of an ounce.

When the feet are kept in the proportion here shown the percentage of lame horses will be reduced to a minimum, for they cannot become lame except by some very infrequent accident. Their chances of getting lame will be in no greater percentage than that of the human family.

Number 4 will give some ideas of proper dimensions of feet by measurement. Height or depth of heels all around, of all four feet should measure comparatively the same. From connection of wall and flesh at 3 straight down dotted line to level floor should measure from about 1 9/16 inches for horses 15 hands, up to inches for horses 16 hands. That is assimulating close to these figures. Depth of foot from 1 to 2 should be about ~~two-thirds (⅔)~~ of the depth from 1 back on an imaginary line running directly through the foot to 3, and this depth from 1 to 2 should measure about 3¼ inches, from connection of wall and flesh at number 1 down to surface of wall at number 2 on a level floor, for horses 15 hands and up to not over 3⅞, to 4 inches for horses 16 hands. Of course these measurements are not to form an infallible rule of dimensions, but they are to govern for feet in ordinarily good condition of health and growth. No foot must be rasped down to these measurements, if in doing so there would be danger of going so low as to leave the sole weak. When the sole yields *slightly*, only, from a *very* hard pressure of *both* thumbs, then the foot surface is pared low enough. If the proper depth of foot can be obtained before reaching to the point where the sole will yield to pressure as explained, all well and good, don't pare down any further. Never pare down to a point that the sole is not strong enough and thick enough to properly protect the foot, for that is what it is placed there for and only so much of it should be removed as is necessary to get the foot at proper depth and so it (the sole) will not bear direct on the shoe.

In a very short space of time the eyes and mind of the owner, the smith, the trainer, etc., will become so educated as to see at a glance what is the proper proportion, angle, etc., as here described, so that no measurements will need to be made.

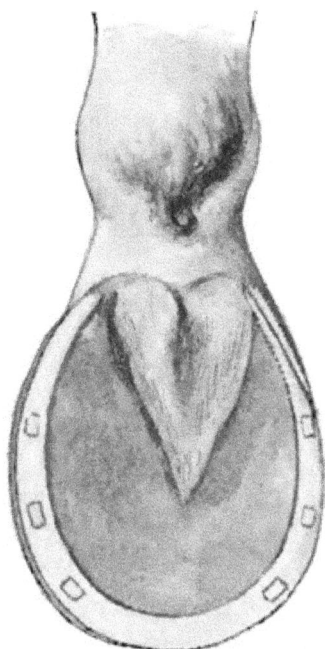

No. 5.

Number 5. This is one of the first feet to call
for an explanation in shoeing, and it is a style
of foot often seen and quite puzzling to the
smith. The cut represents the bottom of a nigh
foot. The tendency of this foot is to grow
faster on the outside than on the inside and to
grow outward and away from the leg, so that it does
not properly support the limb. The rasp should be
used on the outside surface, for a foot that acquires
this tendency of growth will be found, almost invariably, to be deeper on the outside than on the inside.
But do not lower the outside unless it is the deepest.
Also rasp off a little of the wall along the outside
quarter and towards the toe; do this each time the
foot is shod until it gets back into a correct state of
growth. Fit the shoe as shown, driving the last nail
on the outside well back, a little further back than
the nail of the inside. It will be seen that this shoe
fits snug, a shade inside of the wall, all along the outside to the outside toe, even with the wall from this
point around to a shade back of last inside nail, and
from there back to point of heel full, a little outside

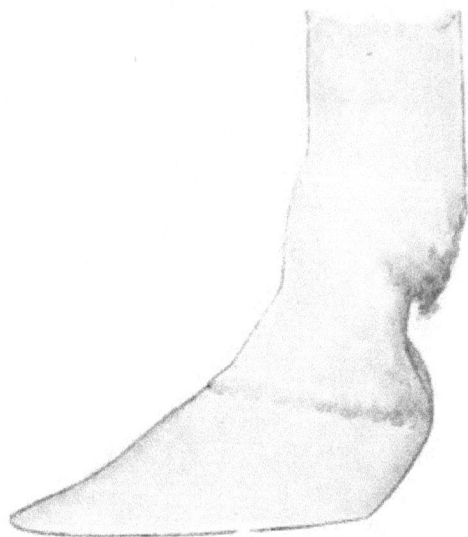

No. 6.

the line of wall. This manner of fitting the shoe
balances the irregular foot and will, consequently,
assist it to regain its proper state of growth. The
support is lessened on the stronger portion of the foot
—the outside—and is strengthened on the weaker
portion—the inside. It will be noticed that the distance of each inside heel of shoe from the crevice of
the frog at the heel, is almost exactly the same, as
near so as can be obtained at first attempt. It will
also be noticed that the distance of each side of the
shoe from the inside of web, at a point on a line with
the point of the frog, will be found to be about the
same, showing that the manner of fitting the shoe
as explained makes the balance of the foot pretty
nearly correct.

Number 6 represents one of the styles of feet to be
found forward, more frequently on many of our
trotting and driving horses, and is placed here to
show more particularly the effect on the ankle joint
of a foot of such incorrect angles. The directions
given with No. 4 will explain how to put this foot in
proper proportion and angle so that it will give the
needed support to the limb.

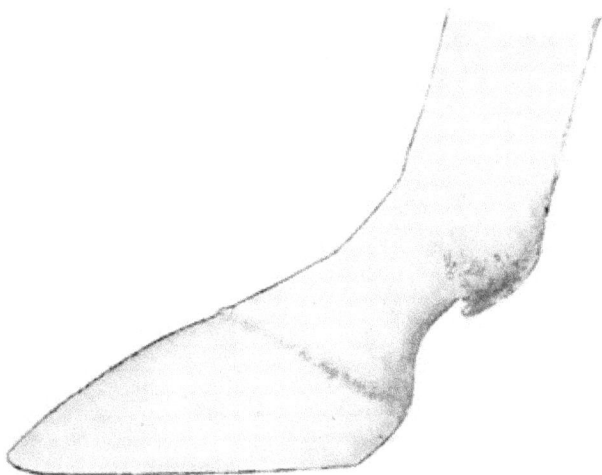

Number 7 is a not infrequent, but on the contrary, a very common form of foot to be seen on many of our horses, more frequently behind, and it is the cause of crooked legs, Curbs, Spavins, Knuckling, etc. In preparing this foot for the shoe, the length and depth of the front of the foot needs attention from the smith with his rasp to remove the surplus. It most likely cannot, usually, be accomplished with the first preparation, that is, it cannot be gotten immediately to absolutely correct proportions, and it is not good judgment to undertake to get it so, at once, as the change would be too positive. Nothing must be taken off the heels of such a shaped foot until they shall have had an opportunity to grow down to below proper depth, so in the meantime until they shall have grown to proper depth, support the heels of the foot with small calkins on the heels of the shoes—*none on the front part, however*—gradually lessen the depth of shoe—at each resetting or re-shoeing—at heels, calkins included, until the foot shall have grown down to proper depth, when shoe with plain shoes of even thickness all

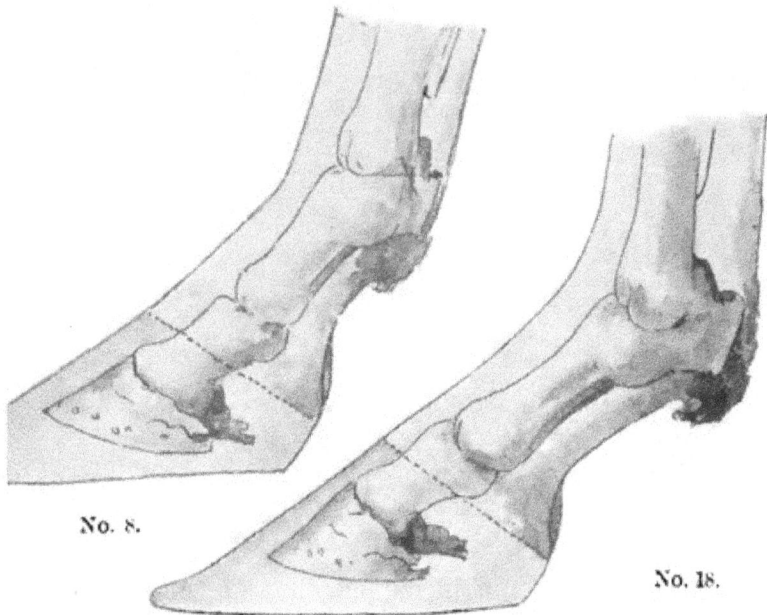

No. 8.

No. 18.

Number 8. This cut shows the form of foot to be found on curby legs and spavined legs; it is often found to be the cause of knuckling on hind ankles, yes, and on fore ones also. It will be seen that the foot is very long and very deep in the front part and of proportionately very little depth at the heels. The base of the structure is wrong, the pedal, or coffin bone, is thrown upward in front from the thickening of the horn below and is canted towards the back; this throws the lower pastern bone—that makes the first joint in the foot in connection with the coffin bone—and the navicular bone as well, out of position, with the result that all of the succeeding joints are more or less "out of whack" in their action.

Number 18 is a cut of foot not dissimilar to number 8, but the angle of the joints is changed at the union of the upper pastern and the main lower bone of the leg so that the ankle is affected. the articulation being comparatively correct above that point, the hock joint is not as likely to be also involved, a trouble more apt to result in the case of number 8. Directions under number 4 will explain how to correct the improper proportions of such feet so as to eradicate and prevent the troubles they cause, and as

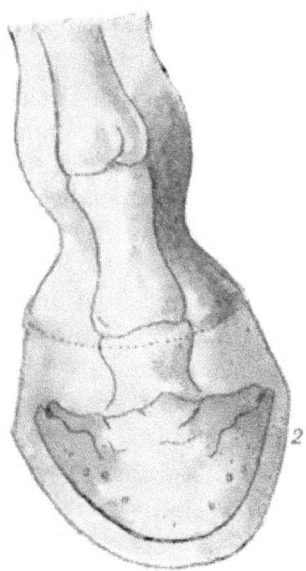

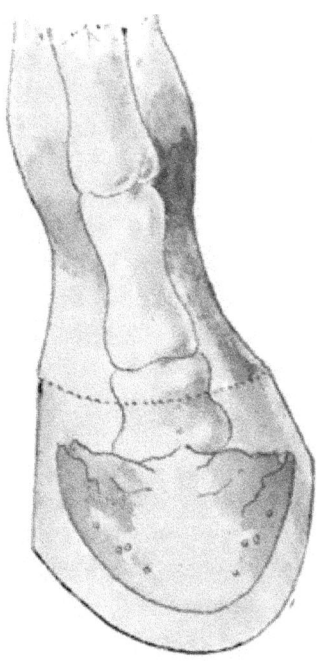

No. 9.   No. 9½.

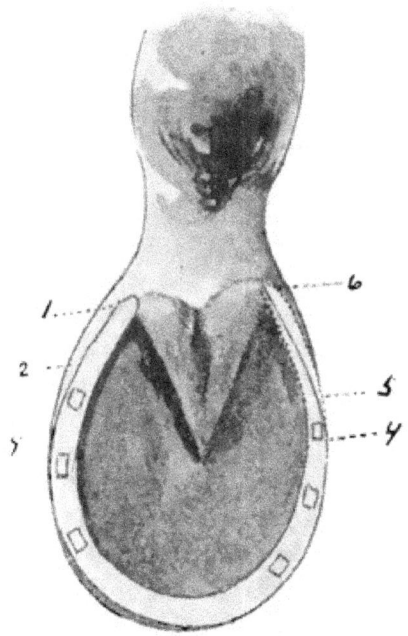

No. 10.

Number 9 is a cut of the "toe out" foot, the "knee banger." The position of the bones forming the articulation are shown here, clearly proving that when it is disturbed at the base it interferes with the whole system of joints throughout the entire leg, and that it is the faulty position of the foot, in its toeing out propensity, that gives the inward slant to the leg and makes the elbow cling in close to the body, just the contrary to that of the "toe in" foot as shown in cut No. 11. Cut No. 10 shows the surface of the same foot (No. 9) and the manner of shoeing it and directions for pairing. Rasp off the surface of wall from 1 to 2, not too much, from 2 to 3 considerable may be taken off with the rasp. Nothing off from 3 to 5—foot surface around inside toe—but from 5 to 6 rasp off to make heel same depth as outside. If these heels are not of sufficient depth—as explained under Number 4—to be in proper proportion, do not rasp off any of the surface wall at the heels. From 4 to 4, after having rasped the surface as already directed, lessen the depth, if it shall require it, equally all around the surface from 4 at about the quarter around the front of the foot surface to 4 at the other quarter. Fit the shoe even with the wall on the outside from 1 to 4, snug, inside the wall, from 4 to 3, even with the wall from 3 to 5 and full from 5 back to point of heel at 6. Before fitting the shoe, the foot should be taken up in front of the leg and the protruding outside toe rasped off from 2 to 3 as shown in cut No. 9. This should be done each time the animal is shod until that toe gets into a regular state of growth and in conformity to the inside one of same foot. Rasp the outside of the wall down to the shoe at from 4 to 3, but do not otherwise rasp the wall on its outside, above or back of the clinches, and do not rasp off any of the enamel to make the foot look "puty."

A foot may "toe out" and the ankle turn in badly from a different cause from the one given here, though such cases are indeed very rare. The "toe in" foot is not apt to be produced—though it might possibly assume that faulty position—from any other cause than that already assigned to it. The toeing out of the foot, the author has seen caused by its being too high at inside heel and outside toe, and not too high on the outside of the foot back of that point, a more frequent cause of the faulty position. (See cut No. 9½). It depends entirely what angle the first bone above the pedal bone assumes as a result of the unbalanced foot. The raising of the inside heel of the foot, not the raising of the surface lay of the foot with some artificial appliance so that it shall be deeper by including it, may, and most generally does, cant the smaller pastern or coronary bone with a decided slant towards the outside line of the limb: per contra, it may cant it so that it will have a most clearly defined inclination to the inside of the leg, making the foot turn out at the toe (" toe out ") while with the other position of the coronary or lower pastern bone it would certainly "toe in." The customary way of shoeing the toeing out, knee-hitting foot is to rasp off the outside of the wall around inside toe and fit the shoe snug around the foot at that point, and fit it full around the outside of the foot. This is all wrong, for it throws the foot out of balance and will assist in keeping up the wrong position of it, for the incorrect articulation that causes the trouble will continue, will in fact. grow to be more emphasized in its errors of action, causing serious trouble to the joints, tendons and muscles, and will cause the foot to wind in more than ever towards the opposite leg.

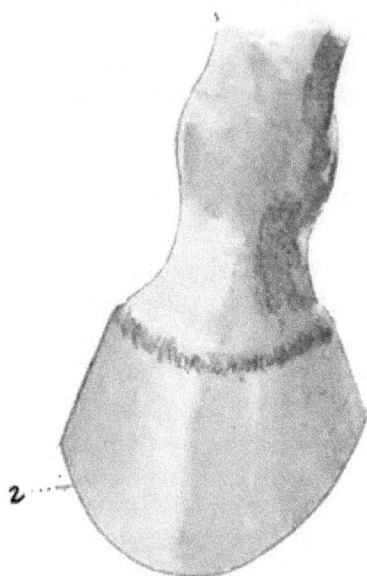

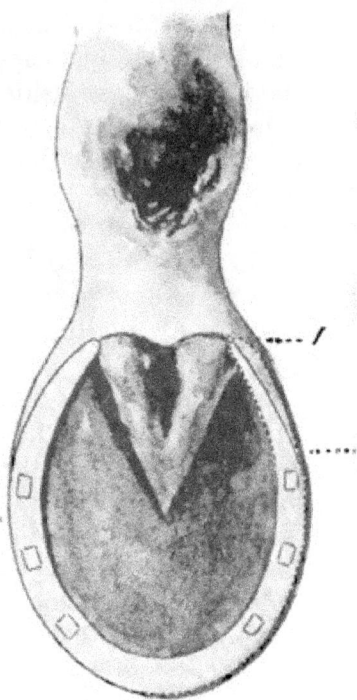

No. 11.

No. 12.

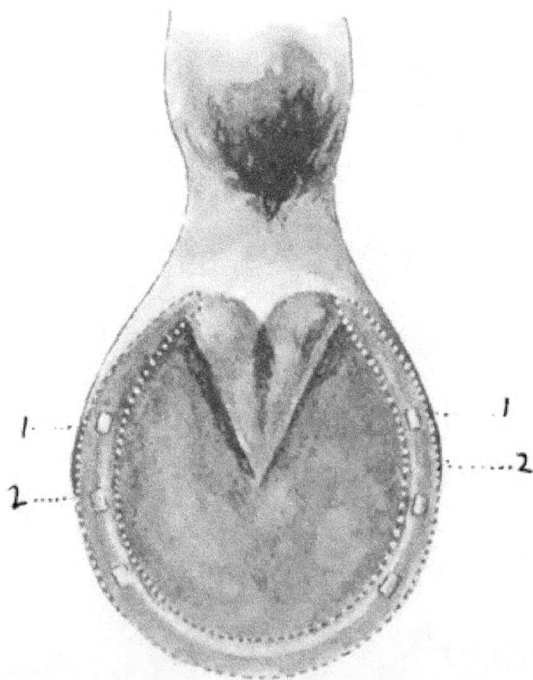

Number 11. A cut of the "toe in" foot. This faulty action is just as fatiguing to the animal as the "toe out" foot, but it is rarely thought of because neither leg is interfered with at any point, by the action of the foot of the opposite one coming against it. This foot requires a preparation for the shoe almost the opposite of the "toe out" foot. The surface wall should be rasped down from 1 all around the inside of the wall of the foot to 2 on outside toe as marked, see cut No. 12. The foot should be taken in front of the leg by the smith and the outside of the wall at the inside toe rasped off to match the outside one, as shown on cut No. 11 from 2 to 3. The shoe should be fitted full from 1 to 3, snug inside the wall from 3 to 2, and full from 2 to 4 and follow the line of the wall from 4 back to point of heel, as shown on cut No. 12.

Number 13 is a cut of the wide foot, about as wide, or wider, as it is long on its surface lay. This is a weak foot and the wall, it will be noticed, is separated from the sole. Many people say a foot cannot be too broad or too wide; they are mistaken, it can, and here is an evidence of it. Such feet are usually found to be broad on the ground surface but narrow and tight at the coronet, a condition that causes an impoverished growth of the wall, and it is evident such is the case, for the wall of such feet will usually be found to be thin as also brittle. In such a foot that discoloration in the sole called "corns" will be often discernable and it arises from the same cause as described under the article on "Corns" which see. The proper manner of shoeing this foot is to fit the shoe evenly under the wall all around, except to have it a trifle full at the heels, if they shall be found to have become curled inward somewhat—not an infrequent condition to be met with in such feet—knock a clip on the shoe inside and outside at the quarters—or at the broadest part of the foot and this is not invariably at exactly what are designated as the quarters—at points designated by space from 1 to 2 and 1 to 2, and have the last nails at the back of the shoes, carried well back towards the heels—just the opposite to that prescribed for placing

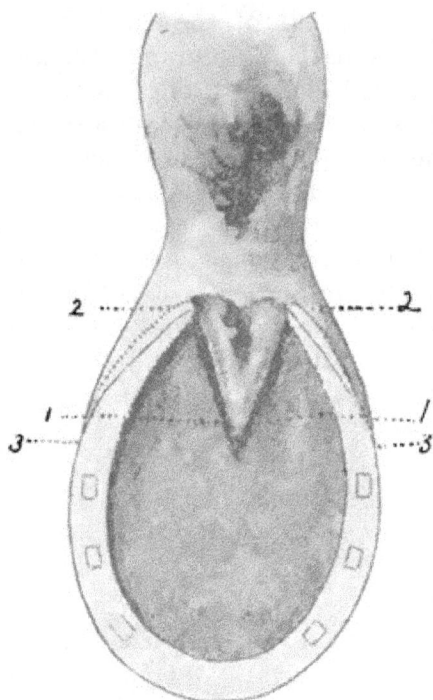

No. 14.

of the nails in the shoe of the one on cut Number 14.
After the shoe is nailed to the foot and before the
smith releases the foot, he should hammer these clips
to the wall so they can get a firm grip. This manner
of fitting the shoe to such a foot will hold it together
at the bottom, giving it increased supporting strength
and it will also loosen it at the coronet, allowing free
circulation of blood, therefore a healthier state of
growth, with the result of a stronger wall and an im-
proved condition of foot generally. Such a foot should
be shod in this manner, for, say about two to three
months—unless it shows marked improvement in a
less time—when it can be shod, most likely, like any
other foot. Always use a shoe of equal thickness
from heel to heel for such a foot.

Number 14 is a cut of a contracted foot. Most generally the heels of such a foot will be found to be
entirely too deep, they should be lowered to the
proper proportion of height, as directed in the measurements given in the explanation of cut No. 4. This
will enable the bones to settle back to their proper

resting place and relieve the tightened condition at the coronet. Lessen the depth of the foot in front if out of proportion. Now then, take the knife—cut given in this work—and clean out the commissures, that is, run this knife back from the point at the frog designated by No. 1, 1, carry the back of the knife close up against the frog, back along its entire length to, and through, between it and the walls at the heels, cut down perpendicular in this way until the sole under the point of the knife along the line of the frog will *give* to a pressure from it (the point of the knife). Care must be taken not to cut through at any point, but this stubborn upper growth of horn must be weakened so that it will not possess strength enough to push up into the vital part of the foot and cause discomfort to the animal at every step; much as it would be to a man walking on the points of the nails of his boot heels that had pushed up through the inner sole and were pressing their points into his foot heel.

The shoe must be fitted as shown : even with the wall all around the front of the foot from 3 to 3, full, outside of the wall, from 3 to 2 and 3 to 2. Have the shoes, from about at 3, 3, back to point of heels beveled, slightly, on the foot surface, towards the outside (the natural inclination of the smith in hammering the shoes at the anvil, seems to be to get the bevel towards the inside, the author has often noticed this), this will give the foot a chance to expand, slightly, each time the foot strikes the ground and will therefore help to get them into a better habit of growth, as nature can now assert herself and help to open this foot out at the heels. The nails should not be driven back any further towards the heels than designated in the cut, the heel then can have nothing to bind it and prevent it from opening, as it will, when the weight is placed on it. Nature will do the rest and no artificial spreaders are either necessary or useful.

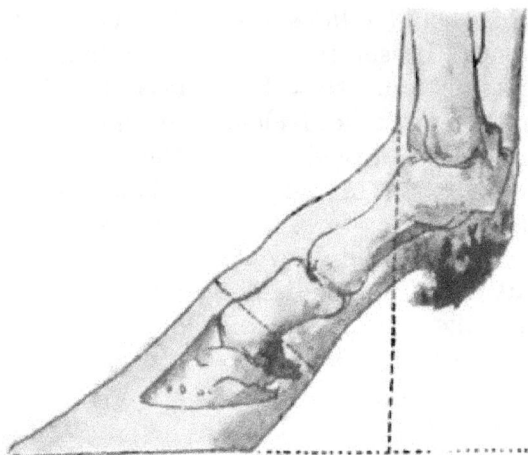

No. 15.

Number 15. This cut is a pretty good likeness of the fore feet of "*Jay-Eye-See*," 2.06¼, and "*Direct*," 2.05½, when the author first took them in hand to shoe. This is a characteristic foot of the family that those two horses are sprung from, for they are Uncle (Jay-Eye-See) and Nephew (Direct). Jay-Eye-See being by Dictator, brother to Dexter, Mr. Bonner's great horse—and he was lame when Mr. Bonner bought him—and Direct by Director, also a son of Dictator. The author says a characteristic foot of the family, so it is. That family had small feet—supposedly an inheritance from the Star mare, the dam of Dexter, Dictator, etc.—but really good feet, and they required a great deal of care to keep them from becoming contracted, and when once they got to be wrong, it was an awful job to get them back again, for they were hardy and unyielding. The author remembers well the trouble he had to get the feet of Jay-Eye-See started to growing, the tightness around the coronet was such that it seemed as though the hide had grown tight to the bones, but it finally yielded and the cast-iron, clever, splendid little fellow, (gamey and perfect in disposition) got to having pretty good feet. The author did not have so much to do with *Direct*, he was a young horse about 6 years it seems, and his feet yielded to treatment more readily than the older one, so that he only shod him twice, the second shoeing being only a few days before he was driven to his record and he has been retired to the stud ever since.

The dotted lines running down the front line of leg to floor are to show more particularly the position of the foot—as regarding its angle to the leg—of Direct more than of Jay-Eye-See, for the latter's pastern was not quite so badly on the slant, though there was not much difference. The latter straightened up from this position so that his foot became to be in quite proper angle to the limb, more so than did Direct's for he was under the charge of the author as to shoeing for about 3 months, whereas he supervised the shoeing of Direct but twice, 3 weeks intervening between the two shoeings.

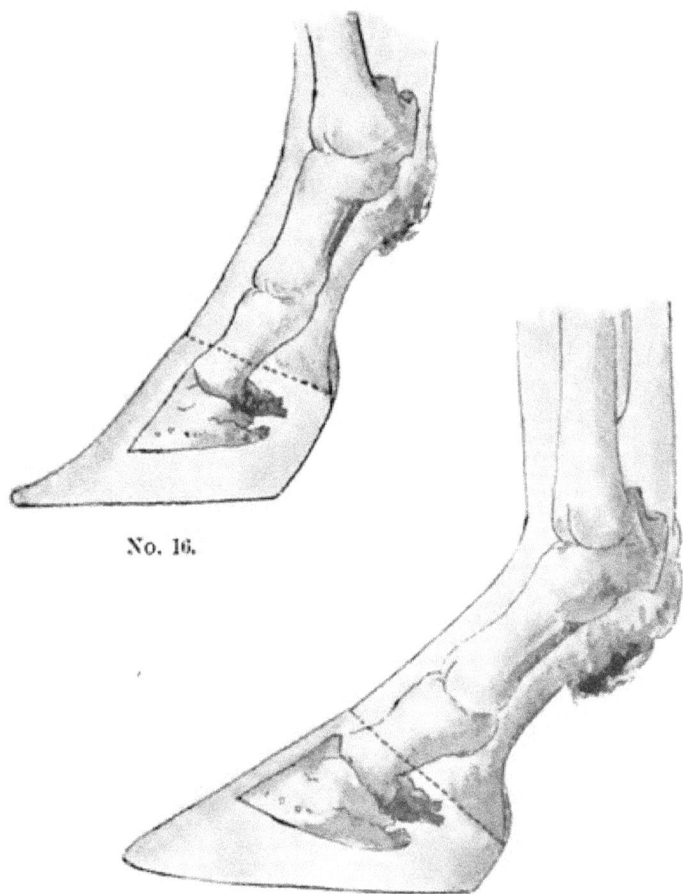

No. 16.

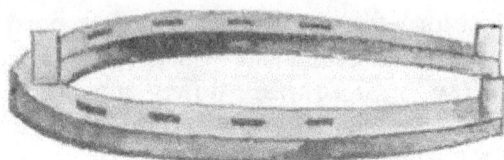

No. 27.

No. 28.

No. 32.

Number 16. This cut shows the position of the bones in forming the faulty articulation caused by an extremely deep heel—yet with a little more depth at front of foot than is proper—and showing that the angle was kept pretty true until it came to the joint formed by the cannon and the upper pastern bone. At this point the proper angle was lost and the result is a case of "Knee Sprung." This is one of the three different causes that will be shown here for a "Knee Sprung" formation. As said before, just which way the cant of the misplaced bones slant can be noticed from the positions of any of the joints that "are out of whack." Putting this foot back to its proper proportions so that the articulation can be made to be smooth and frictionless, as it can, will give nature a chance to remedy the faulty action and the leg will come back to its normal condition again. The author has straightened badly "Knee Sprung" legs on horses as old as 15 to 17 years, and had them keep strong and straight in their limbs, and it can be learned from these pages how easily it is of accomplishment.

Number 17. Exhibits another form of foot found on the "knee sprung" animal. The raising of the front of the pedal bone gives a backward cant to the smaller pastern, or coronary bone, which causes an improper articulation all through the succeeding joints to the knee, and it (the knee) will be uncomfortable in its action also. The pedal bone is thrown out of position by the unwarranted depth of the front of the foot in proportion to the depth of the heels. Also number 22 is still another form; the toe is not deep enough in comparison to the great depth at the heels and the first articulation is seriously incorrect, creating trouble through the succeeding ones. The ankle joint in this case is quite likely, also, to be seriously involved.

These illustrations, like that also of No. 20, are given to show that the improper position of the pedal bone is productive of many and varied faulty articulations, and that the effect of such on the first and suc-

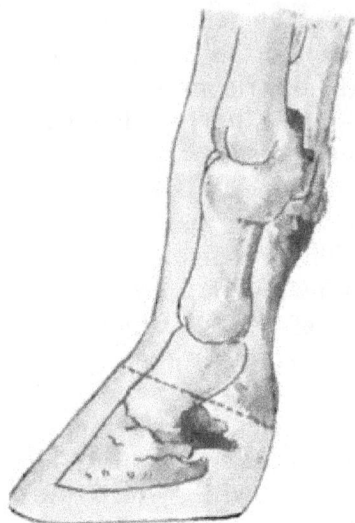

No. 20.

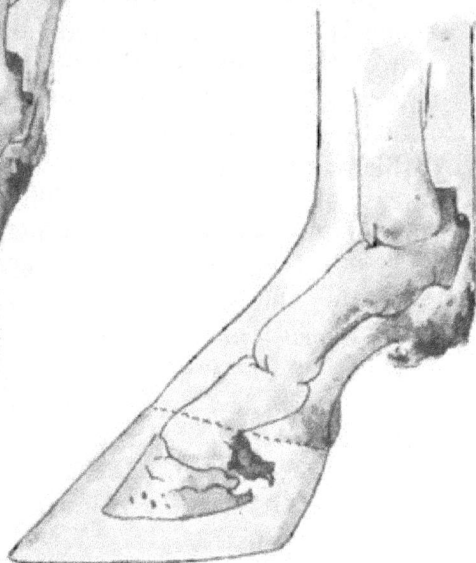

No. 22.

This last, number 20, shows the ankle to be seriously affected instead of the knee, while the foot is of very similar form to that of cut number 22, wherein the knee joint is afflicted. These difficulties are all easily overcome, and the articulation can be made smooth and frictionless by following the directions for form of foot, given in the description under number 4, which see. Don't use irregular thickness of iron to overcome these defects, except in rare cases and as directed in the paragraph, " Balancing the Foot with Rasp, not Shoe." which study carefully.

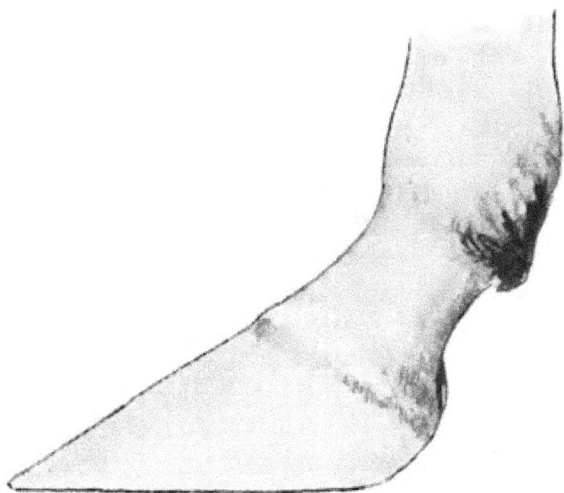

No. 19.

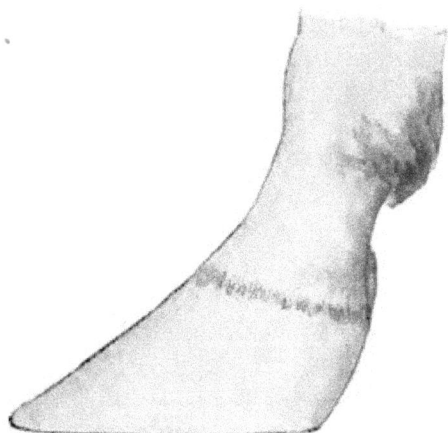

No. 21.

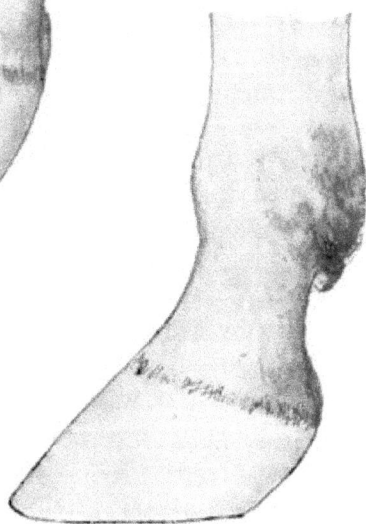

Number 19 shows the form of foot most *frequently* found on the elbow hitter, though numbers 21 and 23 are also forms that will create this bad action but not so frequently as number 19. The enlargement at the ankle on number 23 shows one of the *very frequent* results of the use of toe or side weights. for they force the animal to an action not warranted by the condition of the articulation. 19 and 21 are the sort of fore feet usually found on the forger, and scalping is frequently caused by them, though in the case of scalping the hind feet also are often found to be at fault. The primary cause of the foot getting up to and interfering with the elbow is this: the extra exertion of the flexor tendon required to flex this long toe, is such, that when the foot does leave the ground, it does so with great force and rapidity of action; it is, consequently, by this intense pull on it, carried higher than it would be, if flexed with the ease of the foot of proper proportion and smooth articulation, and which would leave the ground with an easy and pleasing action of the flexors. The author has cured this habit, arising from such a foot as shown by number 19, by lessening the depth of the front of the foot. with the rasp on the surface of the wall and by also using the rasp around the outside of the wall on the front of the foot, removing the elongated toe: after having thus prepared the foot, he would adjust to it a shoe of equal thickness from heel to heel, unless the heels were too low in proportion, in which case he would put slight calkins on the heels of the shoe to increase the depth, (of shoe and foot) to proper angle, until the heels shall have time to grow down to requisite depth, then use a plain shoe. The heel calkins would assist in resting the joints, tendons and muscles, though they would not change the faulty articulation, for that could be done only by growing the foot into proper proportion and angle.

Number 24 exhibits a not infrequent badly formed hind foot—contracted—as is usually the case with the hind foot, contrary to that most frequent with the fore feet—on the outside. For this foot fit the shoe even with the wall all around from inside heel to

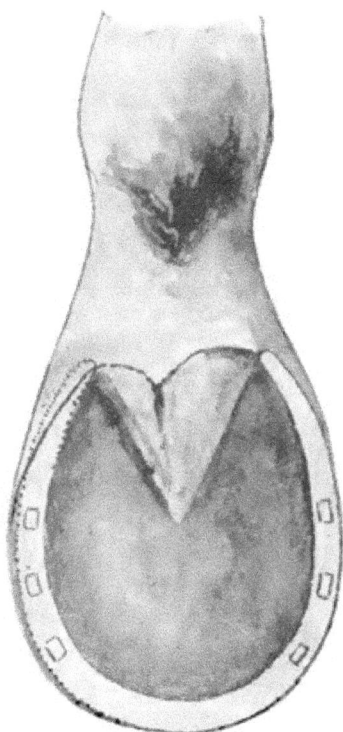

No. 24.

outside quarter, and from there back to point of heel, *full* but *straight* (the inside of the web of each heel should measure about equal distance from the crevice in frog at heel), the shoe *must not be curled outward* on the *outside at heel*, and must not extend back at the heel *beyond the surface lay of the wall of the foot* (unless it is necessary to use scalpers, when both heels should extend back far enough to hold the strap usually used), and the shoe should not extend back further on one side of the foot at the heel than on the other. If this foot is of proper proportion of depth at front and back adjust a plain shoe of even thickness from heel to heel; if, however, that most frequent fault—*more particularly noticeable on the hind feet*—of having the heels of not sufficient depth shall be the condition of them, then, *and then only*, turn up a slight heel calkin, but do not use them when the heels of the feet are of

No. 25.

No. 26.

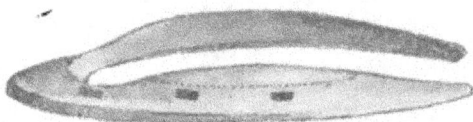

No. 30.

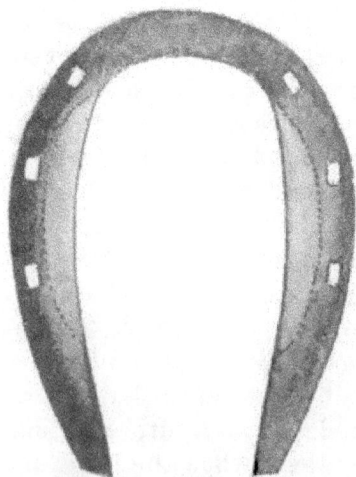

No. 31.

Numbers 30 and 31 show cuts of a shoe for the fore foot which the author has used with great success. This is the only irregular shaped shoe he ever used, under any circumstances, for he does not believe in the use of them, has been successful in his practice without employing them and he cannot see the utility of using shoes that are at variance with the proper level tread of the foot, except that he does *invariably* have the front of the shoe around the toe on the ground surface rasped off about as much as a ten days' use would lessen the depth at the toe of the shoe; he does this to save the animal that much wear and tear of tendons, muscles and joints necessary to produce this lessened toe at surface. Such a shoe is shown in Nos. 25 and 26 and it will be seen to be slightly drawn from about last nail hole back to point of heel. This is the proper shoe to use on sound, well-balanced feet at both ends, before and behind, except the toe need not be worn off on ground surface for hind shoes, for there the full form of shoe is needed to catch the ground well, to assist the propelling of the body and the load. These shoes should be made of steel not *over* five-eighths (⅝) of an inch wide. But to return to No. 30. This shoe is for use on a horse for speed, or for road driving, that is afflicted in his joints, ankle particularly, as also somewhat strained in his muscles and tendons, that is, after getting his fore feet trued and balanced so the cause of the afflictions to joints, tendons and muscles is removed, this shoe will be found to be a resting shoe, as one might say, during the healing process nature is indulging in, after the cause of incorrect articulation has been removed.

The artist failed to show, plainly, the worn off toe at surface in 26.

No. 29.

Farrier's Knife.

Number 29 is a cut of a farrier's knife. This knife is double edged, sharpened the entire length of the blade on one side and only about half the length on the other, as shown by cut; it is especially made to use in cleaning out the commissures in a contracted foot, as described and directed to be done, in treating the contracted foot number 14. It will be noticed that the turn at the point is a sharp one, and that the width over all at point is very slight; it is made so for a purpose, and that is, so that it shall make only a narrow cleaning out of the commissures. The idea of cleaning out these objectionable parts of the deformed foot is to weaken them, so they cannot exert a harmful pressure upward into the vital part of the foot, as already explained. It is not necessary, nor would it be productive of the desired improvement, to dig down into them with a knife broader on the point than the one here shown, for before the ordinary farrier's knife, with its broader point, had reached down into them far enough to give the required relief the wide point would have broken through on each side and the blood would flow. This must be avoided; the commissures must be weakened, but they must not be cut through so that blood would flow. The author can furnish such a knife, upon application, made of good, well tempered steel, with leather blade case, hard wood handle of proper size and shape, for $1.50, sent to any address, postage paid, on receipt of price in anything but postage stamps. The handle is one inch longer than cut, blade same length as shown. *none on hand.*

Draft Horses.

Cut numbers 27 and 28 show a proper form of shoe for use on Draft Horses' feet. It will be noticed that the calkins are not as deep as those usually used and of course will not wear as long, but the saving of strain to the animal with the result of his being better able to more fully utilize his powers, with the much lessened chances of his becoming strained and lamed will more than compensate for the few dollars of extra cost in re-calking his shoes a little oftener than has been the custom. The shoes should not be made so heavy, about one-half to three-fifths of the weight of iron usually used will be found sufficient and if the shoes are made narrower. never *over* one inch in width. but of usual thickness, *they will wear just as long* and the animal's joints, tendons and muscles will be saved much wear and jar in consequence. The nails should be driven at the places in the shoe as on cut, the last nail never further back towards the heel than shown, except in the excessively broad and consequently weak formation of foot, and directions for the placing of them in shoes for such a foot, as also the clips necessary, are described in the directions for shoeing the foot, shown in cut number 13, which see.

One of the most frequent and serious faults in the preparation of the feet of our Draft Horses is that of allowing them to become too deep in the front—often also, too long at the toes—and of too little depth at the heels. This fault is more frequently noticeable on the hind than on the fore feet and causes a great strain to all of the joints, tendons and muscles of the propelling power. Study carefully the discriptions of proportion as given under No. 4, for they are to govern in the preparation of the feet of all horses, and for whatever service used.

Numbers 32 and 33 show cuts of a hind shoe for use more particularly on the race track, for *speed* purposes, though it will be found to be useful for road driving. By examining this shoe carefully it will be observed that while there is a deepening of the shoe at the toe, forming as it were, a toe calkin, whereby the animal obtains a firm grip on the ground at the propelling end, where 'tis needed, the shoe is beveled off from the front part, so that, unlike the calkin, if the foot should interfere with the front foot it would not "cut the quarter" as 'tis called, at any time, but would simply pound it slightly and slide off; at same time, this formation of toe gives the full benefit of a calkin, without, as expressed, any of the disadvantages attaching to the latter. It will be noticed also that the heel calkins are turned up only to balance the shoe so that it shall be of same depth, or thickness at heels as at front of shoe. Friends of the author have informed him that they consider this shoe for hind foot the best speeding shoe ever put onto a horse—and certainly superior to any they have ever used. Many of his friends are "stuck" on the front shoe number 31 also, for the track particularly, as owing to the very slight ground surface, the foot gets an easy blow and then again the resistance is slight, enabling the foot to be flexed with the utmost ease. A shoe of this kind for a horse of 15¾ hands will weigh about 9 to 10 ounces: (they can be made heavier yes, and can be made lighter) but any horse properly balanced in his articulation should be able to trot square and true with that, yes, with much less weight.

The artist made a mistake in number 33, and the drawing does not show the calkin-like shape at toe.

Hind Feet Interfering.

When the ankle of hind leg is interfered with by the foot of the opposite leg, it is because the foot of the leg on which is the afflicted ankle is wrong, it is too high on the inside from the heel to the toe. This gives the leg the appearance of " bow leg " (the contrary condition, too deep on the outside of foot, produces the " cow hocked " formation) and the slant of the foot makes it wind in to find a comfortable lay on the ground in its action, with the consequence, naturally, that it thus gets in the way of the opposite foot in passing and is therefore hit by that foot. The same when both ankles are interfered with, *both* feet are too deep inside. Now it is foolish and not productive of good results—for the sought for remedy cannot be obtained by resorting to such means—to build up the height of the outside, or lower side of the foot, by the use of a shoe thickened on that side, doing this will wrench the ankle joint. The proper way to do is to lower with the rasp the surface of the side that is too high, so that it will match *exactly* in height the opposite of that same foot, and adjust a shoe of equal thickness from heel to heel, except, of course, where calkins are employed and they should be placed on the shoe as directed under the head of Calkins, How to Proportion, which see.

Why Hind Shoes Wear Irregularly.

When the shoes on the hind feet wear away more rapidly on the outside toe—a frequent fault with our trotters and pacers—balance the foot and fit the shoe snug at the outside toe, full—but a straight shoe, no curling outward—at the outside heel and even with the wall all the rest of the way around to the inside heel. This will assist in balancing the action, for the surplus iron at the wearing point will be lessened, therefore less to strike the ground and gradually as the foot, thus assisted in its action, becomes truer in its motion, then the shoe can be fitted evenly all around and will wear evenly.

Growth of Hind Feet.

It is a not infrequent trouble with the hind feet that they get to growing outward at the outside quarter, forming a wing thereon and thus growing away from the proper line of the limb, and therefore not properly supporting it. This outside wing should be gradually rasped off and the shoe fitted snug, close inside of the wall under this irregular growth and a shade full along the inside from toe back to heel. This will weaken the support of the overgrown side of the foot and strengthen the weaker side, thus assisting nature to cure this irregularity of growth, with the result of aiding the foot in its proper support of the limb.

Balance the Foot with Rasp, not Shoe.

When a foot is out of balance, one side higher—or deeper as some may choose to call it—than the other, the lessened depth must not be increased by the appliance of iron to raise that side to the depth of the deeper, but the deeper side must be rasped down on the surface of the wall to match the depth of the lesser, for it must be borne in mind that the improper position of the bones in the foot creating the incorrect articulation cannot be changed to a proper one, except by adjusting the *"balance"* of the *foot itself.* External appliances, such as increased thickness of shoe at one point or another will not and cannot remedy the evil. If, however, the deepest side of the foot is not in itself deep enough, in comparison, so as to be able to stand paring to obtain the required depth, owing to the fact that the opposite side is altogether too much lessened in depth, then a thickened shoe may be used until the feet shall be grown down to sufficient depth to obviate the difficulty by the use of the rasp only. These instructions apply more particularly to the back part of the feet, though of course irregularities in depth at any point on the foot must be remedied by the rasp used on the surface where possible, and not by the use of thickened shoes except as mentioned.

"Hitching," Stringhalt and "Cross Firing."

These three faults, "Hitching," Stringhalt and "Cross Firing," are all caused by unbalanced feet, therefore, an irregular and improper working of the joints, or the muscles, or the tendons, sometimes, and in fact quite frequently, all three may be involved. Hitching can almost invariably be cured in one shoeing; the author has never failed to make the "hitch" disappear with one preparation of the foot, of which he has testimonials establishing the fact. Stringhalt is not as easily cured, but in *all* the cases that have come under the personal treatment of the author, he has cured each and every one of them, and he has invariably found the cause to be an unbalanced foot (with excessive tightness at the coronet, easily corrected) consequently incorrect articulation.

"Cross Firing" is much more easily cured than Stringhalt. In the case of one (or both) hind foot winding in, out of a straight and proper line, the cause can *always* be located *invariably*, in an unbalanced foot, and the instructions contained herein will enable anyone of ordinary intelligence to correct the fault, in fact all three of the above, as well as numerous others of the many faults of incorrect balance to be met with, and to do so without the aid of any mechanical appliances whatever.

Another, though not so frequent a fault as "Hitching" and "Cross Firing" is that of twisting the hind leg or legs, that is, turning the heel of the foot outward by twisting over on outside toe. This also is caused by an unbalanced foot and can easily and surely be stopped, as the author also has learned from his own personal experience in stopping it, generally in one preparation and shoeing of the foot, using only a plain shoe, as he always does.

Runner.

Balancing the *Runner* is accomplished in the same manner as that prescribed for the Trotter and Pacer, notwithstanding they wear plates and not shoes. The author has balanced several of them, though he has not been fortunate enough to form the acquaintance of the owners of any of the more *celebrated* ones, going at that gait, as he has those owning such as go at the trot and pace. The Runner can be so balanced in his feet as to make the articulation so smooth and frictionless, the action therefore, of the joints, tendons and muscles so equalized, that it will be impossible for a "break-down" to occur, except by the rarest and most infrequent of accidents. He may be run to a standstill, he may be jumped over hurdles and ditches with impunity, but he cannot "break down", for there will be no *unequal strain on the joints, tendons or muscles*, the *primary causes* of *all "break-downs"*.

As the author has had considerable experience in driving horses, covering many years, he has been repeatedly asked questions about check reins, etc.

The above cut shows a checking rig—partly the invention of the author—used by him for past 20 years on different horses of varied dispositions and with satisfactory results in all cases. They could all go faster and steadier than with any other manner of checking. It gives the animal "a fine mouth." It is the best by all means, for rigging a team for style and comfort of driving. While this arrangement gives more perfect control of the animal in case of fright, accident, etc., it is at no time oppressive or in the least annoying to him. For breaking and driving colts it is invaluable.

It was a rig *exactly* like this that the great **"Alix"** wore when she made the world's record, **2.03¾**, and *after the author of this work had directed the preparation and shoeing of her feet.*

"Balancing the Trotter."

Copy of a letter written by the author and published in the American Horse Breeder of Boston.

" I am in receipt of your favor asking me to write for you an article on the above subject. I will try to give you some points that may be of interest, but as horses' feet differ so widely, it would take a volume of good size to give a set of rules that could sufficiently cover the many types of different feet, so that it might be found of practical benefit to owners and breeders, and they are the class of people who might be interested, if I can command attention from any who take an interest in the horse and how to balance his action. Drivers and trainers have rarely any use for information. They "know it all," and I do not write for their edification.

One thing to start with is that I never use any peculiar shoe or any artificial mechanical contrivance to balance the gait of the trotters. I do all my work in the way of balancing on the feet themselves, and adjust a shoe that carries out perfectly that balance, for pacers as well as trotters.

I notice that all of the so-called practical horseshoers explain how to cure this and that trouble of irregular action by the use of some sort of a shoe, made in an irregular manner. Very few of the designs described are at all novel or new to me, and not a single one of them is fit or necessary to put on the foot of a horse in order to correct the fault it is sought to remedy.

Strange shoes may temporarily change the action of the knee hitter, the elbow hitter, the forger, the sculper and other wrong and deviating gaits, but they will not cure the animal of any of these faults, if the foot that offends be still allowed to remain in the faulty position that caused the irregularity complained of. Another objection to the use of such inventions is that most of them do actual harm to the joints, tendons and muscles of the animal. It must be borne in mind that the instinct of the horse suggests to him the action or gait that is the easiest for him to use, and such he will invariably employ.

Should the motion be wrong and not in proper rhythm, and the animal is forced to adopt by the use of mechanical appliances any other line of action, without the faulty articulation being corrected, he will do so at the cost of injury to some parts of the motor power, just as sure as it is true that the sun "do rise and set."

In my younger days the perfectly-proper foot for all horses was one that on its surface lay would make an almost perfect circle, barring the break at the heel. It was claimed by such people as Goodenough, the inventor of the shoe bearing his name, that the foot should be as broad as it was long. At the time he came on the carpet, about 30 years ago, high heels and short toes were in vogue as the general rule for the front feet for the light-harness horse. Yes, in fact, for all horses that were shod. Goodenough—and I knew him intimately—was the first man at that time, 30 years ago, who called my attention to horse-shoeing for my own horses.

His whole system consisted in cutting down the heels to get "frog pressure." He knew nothing about the proper proportioning of the foot. He also knew absolutely nothing about what was a fair proportion of depth for the front of the foot, as compared with the depth of the hind part of it, and that was why many horses became lame after wearing the shoe that he invented. The fault was not with the shoe, for that has its merits, but it was this constant hacking away at the heels and leaving the front of the feet all out of proportion as to depth and length.

I speak of this, as it leads up to the practice now in vogue. Almost all drivers and trainers have the feet of their trotting horses too long and too deep in the front of the foot, in proportion to the height or depth, whichever term may seem to best convey the idea intended, at the heels. This is one of the most frequent causes of unbalanced gaits. The low-heel trouble is more frequently to be seen on the hind than on the fore feet, and is one of the causes of crooked, cow-hocked legs, which produce curbs, spavins, etc. Then on this unbalanced foot is placed that most nonsensical and absurd thing, it is not worthy to be called shoe, the long outside winged heel for the hind feet, longer than the foot and running away off to the outside like a sled runner. This contrivance, coupled with the unbalanced foot on which it is placed, has made more lame horses behind than most any and all other contrivances that the genius of man has yet devised.

Why put on such a thing? What is it for? Why put this wing on the shoe? There is no foot where it is put. It supports (?) nothing; it is only in the way and gives the animal an unnatural tread and an uncomfortable one. Why put iron in such a useless abundance where there is no foot? Don't do it. There are feet and feet. The old-fashioned round foot spoken of was a weak one. Many times, yes, quite frequently, it would be found upon examination of the bottom of the foot that the wall had separated from the sole. Widening the foot out this way caused the walls to spread apart away from their proper position as a means of support to the pedal bone, consequently the main support to the limb was weakened and the principal and most important articulation seriously interfered with. This style of foot was cultivated most frequently for the fore feet. The hind ones would be lower at the heels.

In shoeing such a foot the shoe should follow closely the wall from heel to heel, all around, and at the quarters, both inside and outside, a clip should be struck on the shoe and the nails allowed to be driven well back toward the heels, which never should be allowed in a foot of fairly correct proportions, and the clips hammered to a proper, good resting place before the foot is placed on the floor from the smith's hands. This practice of shoeing such feet will gradually bring them together more, as it were, and make them incline to a healthier proportion of growth, and thus will the support be regained and an important point in balancing the trotter be gained also.

Horses with such feet as described for the fore and hind ones will be found standing with their fore feet well back under the girth and their hind ones standing under their loins. Very little space will be noticeable between the fore and hind feet on the ground lay of them. In old times this used to be "the thing." It used to be remarked, "I like to see a horse stand with all his four feet well under his body."

Now, a good judge of horses wishes to see the hind legs stand straight down under the quarters, so that a plummet attached to a string held at the point of the hock will make the string lay against the back part of the leg, all the way down to the fetlock joint. When a horse stands this way not much fault can be found with the "balance of the trotter," as far as his hind action is concerned. Then, with the front feet in proper proportion and angle, the leg will stand plumb and straight from the shoulder down, and not with the feet standing back under the girth.

The only way to "balance the trotter" is to have his feet truly balanced and in proper proportion and at proper angle to the limbs they support, so that the articulation will be as near frictionless as possible. With this condition maintained the animal's instinctive action will be even and true, with a perfect rhythm.

The fad nowadays with nearly all drivers and trainers is the long and deep foot in the front part and an all-out-of-proportion, low heel. This manner of proportioning the feet is ruining our trotters faster than we can raise and educate them. If the smith cannot balance the foot any other way, let him measure it with a set compass, so that he may be enabled to have one side exactly the same height as its opposite of the same foot. In this way one of the most important points in "balancing the trotter" will have been gained.

Now as to the proportion and angle of the foot to the limb it supports. I have to stop here. I know of no infallible rule to lay down for this, except that the measurement of the front of the foot from centre at the coronet to the surface lay of the foot should be about 65 per cent. of that of the depth of it, measuring from the same point at coronet back along an imaginary line drawn straight through the center of the foot, from the point of commencement at the coronet, back to a line drawn across the heels, and the judgment of the intelligent owner and breeder must come in now to govern. He must get the foot of the proper depth and length in front and proper depth at the heels, so that to his eyes it shall look as though it was set under the limb in artistic comfort.

When the feet are apparently well balanced and in proper proportion and angle to the limbs, rasp off the edge of the wall at surface and drive the horse a few days barefooted. It will not hurt him or hurt his feet, for the feet when sound and healthy (if the soles have been left intact, as they should be) do not need any protection of iron nailed on to them, it matters not how hard the road-bed may be. If his gait is smooth and even at the trot without shoes you have got him balanced.

Now, then, shoe him with exactly the same weight of iron on each of the four feet. That is, make the hind shoes of the same bar of steel (it is better than iron for shoes for many reasons) that the fore ones are made of. Then if the hind feet are a little smaller, as they sometimes are, the shoes will be all right. Why should you put more weight on one foot than on the other if your trotter is perfectly balanced in his gait barefooted? There is no reason why you should do so, and I have balanced a great many trotters and pacers in just this way, and always successfully.

I trued and balanced the feet of a colt recently for a friend of mine near Chicago. This colt is a yearling, a good, strong one, speedy, and after I fixed his feet, pure gaited. I told this young man not to put any shoes on him at all, for what little driving I wished him to give him he would not need them. I wanted him walked, and walked fast, very fast. It is the best muscle-making exercise that can be given to a horse or colt. Well, there was a smart smith down at this place, and he bet he could shoe this colt so that he would pace.

My friend had implicit confidence in my ability to true and balance his colts, and he knew also that all their irregularities of gait had disappeared entirely after I had done so, so he bet the blacksmith, and how do you suppose he shod this colt so as to make him pace? He put some eight-ounce shoes on the hind feet and three-ounce shoes on the fore, and he could not make him do anything but trot. He then took off the fore shoes, left his fore feet bare, and still kept the shoes on the hind feet, and yet he would do nothing but trot.

The smith paid his bet and gave it up, but he said: "That man Hall beats anything I ever saw. I never saw a horse before I could not make pace by shoeing him that way." He couldn't this one, because the horse's instinct, which guided him to go at the easiest gait, demonstrated to him that that gait was the trot. I have always claimed, and do still claim, that the pacing gait is not the natural one. I will grant that the instinct of action at the pacing gait may be, at times, inherited, but it more often comes from the articulation being unbalanced. The reason we have more pacers now in proportion to what we used to have is simply because the race tracks give good purses for them to contend for, and therefore breeders and owners do not try to make the young things trot when they are at all inclined to pace, as they formerly did when they were of less value for racing purposes.

One strong argument in my favor is, to my mind, the almost absolute disuse of the hock joint at the pacing gait. What was that very important joint put at the propelling end for, if it were not to assist the animal in his movements? So I call a pacer an unbalanced trotter.

Now one thing more about the preparation of the foot for the shoe, and I reckon I am about through. Don't remove the sole from the foot any more than just the width of the shoe, so that the shoe will not rest on it. For winter shoeing, leaving the sole untouched, prevents to a large extent "balling," and in summer it offers a protection against picking up stones and a strong resistance to nail penetration. Always use narrow-webbed shoes, not over five-eighths of an inch wide.

If the feet are trued and balanced, make the shoes of even thickness all around from heel to heel, for all four shoes for each horse. With a perfectly-levelled and balanced hind foot, why put calkins on the heels of the shoes. Don't they throw the feet out of balance? Then, as the front of the shoe wears away faster than the hind part of it, is not the lay of the foot getting more and more off the level all the time?

For myself, I always put the shoes on all feet, drawn a shade, only a shade, from last nail hole back to point of heel, just to assist in equalizing the wear as much as possible. The last nails in the shoes on either side should never be put further back than on a line with the wing of the pedal bone under any circumstances, except as already explained for the foot that is too wide. So it would seem that one of the surest, safest and therefore best ways of balancing the trotter and pacer would be to true and balance his feet, round off the edges of the walls so that the feet will not break in coming in contact with the ground, and drive him a few days barefooted.

If he is balanced, that is, even and true-gaited bare footed then shoe him as directed. For it must be borne in mind that the only practical way to "balance the trotter" is to true and balance his feet and make them be in proper proportion and in proper angle to the limbs they support. In no other way can the gait be made even and true and in perfect rhythm, except at risk of injury to the joints, muscles, tendons, as a natural result of artificial appliances to the feet and limbs, in order to force the animal to an action that the position of his joints does not fit him to take."

More insight on this subject will be obtained by following the directions for preparing and shoeing the foot contained in this work.

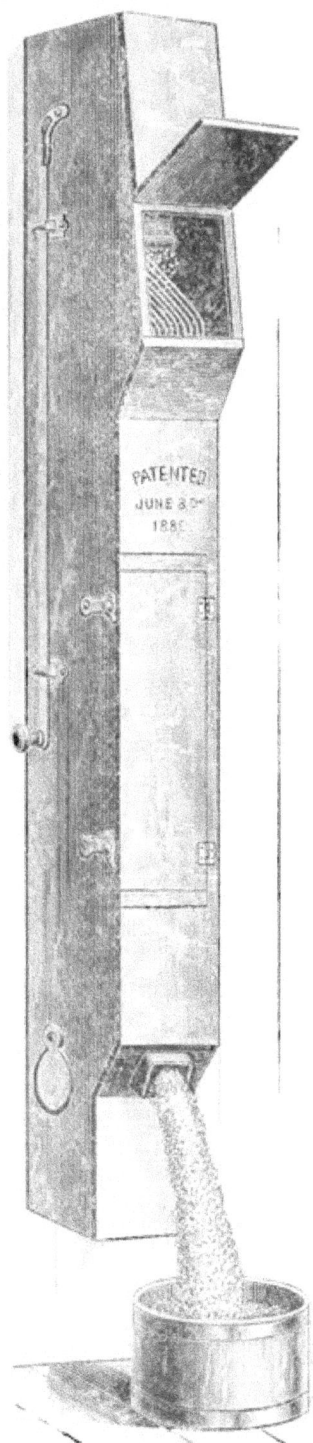

A Fact Worth Knowing!

That Liverymen Using a

Kasper Self-acting Oats Cleaner

in their stables have

GOOD SOUND HORSES

and save money in their feed bill.

Send for a Cleaner on 30 days' trial, and if not satisfactory return it at my expense.

MEDAL AND DIPLOMA

AWARDED BY

World's Columbian Exposition.

Any imitation or infringement of this device will be promptly prosecuted . . . .

Over 14,000 in use.

Send for Descriptive Circular to

THOMAS WHITFIELD,

SOLE OWNER
AND MANUFACTURER

369 Wabash Ave.,

CHICAGO.

Directions in Case of Special Enquiries
for Shoeing (this and opposite page).

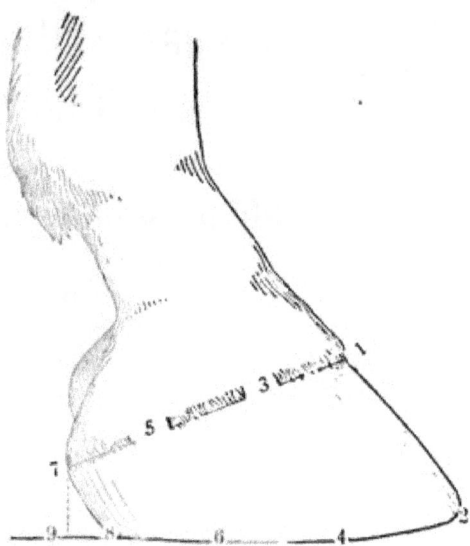

Take a *Set* compass (blunt one point of compass, to use at top of foot, at 1, 3, 5 and 7), and measure each of the four (4) feet from 1 to 2. Then measure in same manner from 3 to 4, 5 to 6, 7 to 8 and 7 to 9, both inside and outside, *separately,* of each of the four (4) feet. Send me these measurements in inches, and fractions of an inch, to a sixteenth of an inch. The surest and most accurate way to take the last four measurements (3 to 4, 5 to 6, 7 to 8 and 7 to 9) is to commence with the nigh (left) fore foot, first measure it on the *outside*—carefully—at the four points designated. Then take the nigh hind foot, the same way, then the off hind foot, then the off fore foot. Then, commencing again at the *nigh* fore foot, go from foot to foot as directed and measure the *inside* of each of the four feet. Be careful to put down *plainly* on a piece of paper, each measurement *separately* and *distinctly* as fast as taken. Don't take a second measurement until first has been put down. Place the blunt point of the compass at *exactly* the point where wall of foot and flesh join, (at 1,3,5 and 7) and the sharp point at wall at surface.

Directions in Case of Special Enquiries
for Shoeing (this and opposite page).

Toeing In.

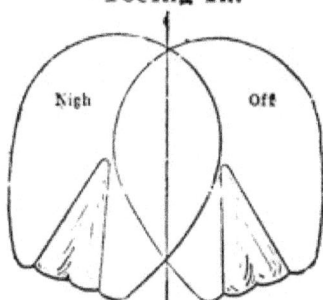

Nigh   Off

Toeing Out.

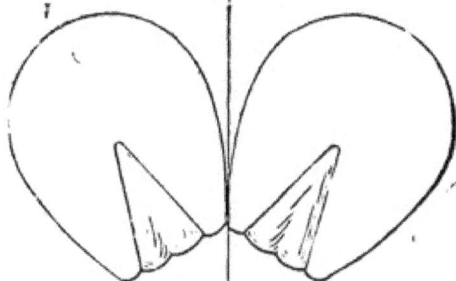

CORRECT POSITION.
Toeing straight to the front, both before and behind.

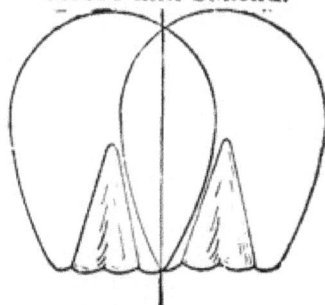

Place horse—barefooted—on a piece of paper on a level floor, standing him as natural as possible. Draw a line through the center of paper, as shown here. Place point of inside heel of each of the four (4) feet on this line. Then sketch around the surface of the foot on the paper with lead pencil, and send sketches to author's address. Keep pencil perpendicular.

Send height—in hands—of each animal, also age, being careful to place age and height against the name